CONSULTING INTERVIEWS GUARANTEED!

© Copyright 2015 – Andrew Morssen

ISBN-13: 978-1514867822
ISBN-10: 1514867826

All rights reserved: This document is geared towards providing exact and reliable information in regards to the topic and issue covered. The publication is sold with the idea that the publisher is not required to render accounting, officially permitted, or otherwise, qualified services. If advice is necessary, legal or professional, a practiced individual in the profession should be ordered.

- From a Declaration of Principles which was accepted and approved equally by a Committee of the American Bar Association and a Committee of Publishers and Associations.

In no way is it legal to reproduce, duplicate, or transmit any part of this document in either electronic means or in printed format. Recording of this publication is strictly prohibited and any storage of this document is not allowed unless with written permission from the publisher. All rights reserved.

The information provided herein is stated to be truthful and consistent, in that any liability, in terms of inattention or otherwise, by any usage or abuse of any policies, processes, or directions contained within is the solitary and utter responsibility of the recipient reader. Under no circumstances will any legal responsibility or blame be held against the publisher for any reparation, damages, or monetary loss due to the information herein, either directly or indirectly.

Respective authors own all copyrights not held by the publisher.

The information herein is offered for informational purposes solely, and is universal as so. The presentation of the information is without contract or any type of guarantee assurance.

The trademarks that are used are without any consent, and the publication of the trademark is without permission or backing by the trademark owner. All trademarks and brands within this book are for clarifying purposes only and are the owned by the owners themselves, not affiliated with this document.

Table of Contents

Chapter One *1*

Chapter Two *5*

Chapter Three *12*

Chapter Four *20*

Chapter Five *23*

Chapter Six *29*

Conclusion *38*

CHAPTER ONE

Understanding Consultancies and the Interview Selection Process

For some reason, people invest too much of their valuable time and effort into studying for interviews that they may never have. Also, it is important to understand that some of the interviews that they believed that they had, were merely an illusion; firms interviewed them, but had almost no intention of hiring.

To make my point absolutely clear, consultants get promoted roughly every two years, sometimes in exceptional cases it can happen annually. So when there are available positions in senior roles they are almost always filled internally. Any position you apply for has to be up at highest level of Assistant Manager, unless you come from another consulting firm or you are really good at what you do in your domain and considered as a Subject Matter Expert.

When there is a role available even though it will certainly be filled internally, it is advertised and the recruitment staff interview some of those candidates even though they know none of them will be hired. It's unfortunately a no-win situation for most candidates. This is why I earlier said that some interviews candidates think they had are merely an illusion.

There are, of course, exceptions to this, such as MBA campus recruitment. These applications actually have a slightly higher chance than average of being successful. But your chances of being hired are still insignificant, unless you are from INSEAD and applying to Strategy& (former Booz), HBS and applying to McK, or those business schools who are listed with top consulting firms. To put it simply, such positions are in very limited supply, and no Business School will be able to fast-track you. Therefore, you don't need to spend your precious time on cracking case studies until you are actually scheduled for an interview. You can worry about this later.

Consultancy Core Skills

Another misconception in the industry is that you already need to be an excellent consultant to get a job at consulting. That's also far from the truth. Consulting at its core is three things combined: problem solving ability with a solid methodology, excellent communication skills with outstanding speaking and writing skills, and dedication to success. If you possess that latter two, employers will be willing to teach you the first one.

Problem solving essentially involves following the methodology of the employer you work with. At its core, identifying the actual root cause of the problem, separating this from the symptoms, identifying and evaluating the alternatives, ranking the potential solutions, picking the best alternative, and developing KPIs to measure the success can be considered a sound enough methodology.

You need a new approach to the entire job hunting business. The methods you have used so far evidently haven't worked, as you have ended up having to read my book. Good for you! This will not be a book that comes from an academic who has probably never had any consulting experience, but somehow has the audacity to actually teach it. This happened to me at my business school. I was taught strategy consulting from an academic, and later I found out that numerous things he told me were completely outdated and mostly irrelevant.

The Odds Against You

There are over 1,000 regular job applications per day to consulting in PwC MENA which is where I work as a Manager in Strategy consulting. Can you guess how many get invited for interviews with a hiring manager? Pretty much zero! Yes, you heard me right. Not even 1 person out of 1,000 applicants per day get a chance to be interviewed. When I found out about this it shocked me. I found it almost unethical. I discovered this after a series of calls from our regional partner asking for us to refer candidates. The first time I heard, I thought to myself, "Okay, since we are good consultants he probably thinks that people we are acquainted with are also good, and thus he trusts us to submit resumes". Then, I heard it again and again, and I realized that all the partners in the firm were constantly on the look out for talent.

I started questioning this process, and came across the HR partner in the office, and asked her how many applicants were received daily. Her answer was "hundreds, if not a 1,000 per day".

Now this is seriously messed up. There is a broken link somewhere. How is it possible that on one hand we are craving for good talent, burning out existing consultants due to a lack of talent, and on the other there is a sincere desire to hire people and thousands of applications which are going to waste? Something somewhat unethical was going on, or the hiring processes were massively ineffective.

What I decided to do next was discuss the issue with my friends at other consultancy firms. To my surprise, it was no different. The same problem existed there. Over 350,000 applications per year, and only a few make it into these organizations. The vast majority, in fact over 99.99%, simply don't get a look in.

> *Not even 1 person out of 1000 applicants per day get a chance to be interviewed.*

At this point, I will want you not be the person who reads endless times books published by academics who have never been there teaching you how to do things. These often involve Myers Briggs-type character analysis, deal with consulting tools that are vastly outdated, and which tell you how to approach a problem without ever having actually encountered serious corporate problems in real-life. In this book, I will speak as if I am your mentor, and document the entire process in the same tone. The title of the book is its modus operandi. I am here to help you get a job at a major consulting company, or at least almost guarantee an interview, not teach you how to do consulting, or format your resume (although I provide very good advice on that front as well!).

CHAPTER TWO

The Image of the Consultant and the Reality

I am sure you have already encountered a management consultant with a $1,000 suit, striding around the airport with his fancy laptop bag with a swagger that indicates that he has just finished creating the earth and is on a very important mission to create a new planet. He is evidently extremely busy and constantly on call with his subordinates, and perpetually uses sophisticated words such as; proliferate, enablers, drivers…

Well, although I have been in management consulting for the past decade, and my career flourishes from year to year, I was lucky enough to segregate myself from people like these and use any opportunity I have had to ensure that no-one is promoted with this attitude. If you ask what these people actually do, they will most probably state that they solve the most important problems of corporates and governments. The reality is that consultants do so many different things.

In 2014 alone, I delivered over 32 projects, with 3 to 5 projects in parallel at any given time. I have done everything from strategy benchmark assessments for a regional Ministry, to a PMO set up for a large corporate, alongside a vision analysis for another corporate, to a strategy implementation.

Of course, I solved many problems along the way, seeking the most tangible value-adds for short, medium, and long-term benefits, maximizing returns. Thus, when somebody asks what I do, the words "solving the most important problems for the greatest companies in the world" is far from what I normally divulge.

Ultimately, we do basically everything that management personnel in a large company does. The only difference is that my job and team keeps on changing every 4 weeks to 6 months. When I get engaged with a client, I am never expected to get onboard and miraculously solve a problem that they couldn't sort out on their own. This is never the case, contrary to what some consultancy firm employees may assert.

Identifying a Joint Solution

Your client is your biggest asset in enabling you to identify a solution jointly. No MBA degree will give you enough experience or expertise to come into a field and tell your client what to do. We develop solutions together with clients. Most of the time, large companies do not have a diligent or logical approach towards a particular situation or they are too close to the picture. That's what we are good at. That is our job. Our thought processes are so highly trained that we can guide a team towards a solution. Ultimately, you aid people not direct them.

That's why PwC and Deloitte are the largest professional services firms in the world. They work with clients to solve problems with their approach, research capabilities, and past experience.

The Wide Knowledge Base

Perhaps another quality that I need to mention at this point which is really important in consulting is high intellectual capacity and a wide knowledge base. I am sure you have heard of the saying "knowing a mile wide, but an inch deep". That should be your entire ethos. You need to know and understand many things, but not necessarily to a deep level. Just know that they exist, what they do, and why they are important. Then when you need to have a deep understanding of a particular subject, you can easily research it.

This approach helps you to connect dots more easily. For example, a solution to one of the recent problems we encountered for a client ended up being a form of bio-chemistry technology that I had previously read about. As soon as it occurred to me that this may potentially address the issue, I immediately engaged the subject matter experts within the firm and developed the perfect solution. Had I not read about it in an article a couple of years ago, we would have had an extremely difficult time in connecting the dots, as no other team member, including the client, had any idea that bio-chemistry could be even remotely close to what we needed.

Some problems are not solved with 7S, 5P, or whatever digit-letter combo consulting tool. You just need to know things. My intention in this book is again not to dive into the nuts and bolts of consulting. I am only mentioning things that you can leverage for your interviews.

The Life of a Consultant

I also tried my best not to get into the topic of whether consulting is for you. But I can't resist mentioning that travelling is not as fun as you may think! After years of repetition, hotel rooms become dungeons. If you are in your twenties, it is not difficult to find the motivation you need to keep going and pushing, but once you hit your thirties (I am 34), things become really difficult. You are probably married, perhaps with kids. Your priorities in life change dramatically; you simply want to spend more time with your wife and kids.

However, the irony is that nice employers will keep sending you all over the world so that you don't have the opportunity to enjoy all of the perks that come with nice compensation. Worst of all is that there is no end to it. Everyone works very hard. Juniors to prove themselves, seniors to get a shot at being a partner. A director can stay as a director for decades without ever becoming a partner. Even if you become a partner, your workload and travel frequency doesn't really diminish. You can't say that "once I am a partner, I won't be travelling that much". That is simply not the case. Partners work as hard as anyone, if not harder. They are extremely driven, only to add more value to clients…a million dollar profit share also helps!

However, there is a positive flip side to this coin as well. I love consulting. As a character, I am easily bored at work. If it's a project which lasts for more than three months then I itch for a change. I can't imagine myself working for the same company in the same function, even with a different seniority, for more than two years. That would be the ultimate torture for me. I am sure I couldn't survive. My motivation would disintegrate, and I would either get fired or resign for another role in a different company, only to find myself in the same situation again after two years. That's just one of the great perks of being a consultant.

Another perk that I highly value is when we occasionally do "good work". One of my recent clients was a regional ministry of a country in the Middle East. We created incredible programs that benefited hundreds of thousands of needy people. With the benefit of hindsight, I am proud to say that I was of one of the five people who developed that program, implemented it on behalf of our clients, and successfully rolled it out to beneficiaries. We touched the lives of hundreds of thousands of people. We made it possible because we came up with efficient models to ensure that it was financially sustainable to allocate such funds. Not many people can say that they have touched the lives of others in such a way. Those beneficiaries have no idea who we are, but we helped them massively. They don't need to know. I know. And, that's more than enough.

Of course, not all of our client engagements are like that. We may also end up delivering work for some evil investment bank that will acquire a poor SME to break it into pieces, fire everyone without any compensation, and sell the IP rights. It is what it is.

Also, remember the prestige that comes with the job. Everybody looks up to consultants, especially to the ones that work at big firms. Working for a big consultancy firm is like getting a job insurance for life. Once you are a consultant at a big firm in a good position, you will most likely never be unemployed again. It's usually just a matter of picking the best offer.

Take a quick look at the LinkedIn profiles of ex-consultants and you will garner this impression yourself very quickly. Never having to worry about being unemployed ever again, even if the greatest recession episode 2 plays out; who wouldn't want that kind of insurance? If your consultancy dreams work out, then you will find yourself very much at the top of the food chain. You may find a lesser paying job, but you will always be the preferred candidate, at least on resume.

Thus, the advantages of becoming a consultant are pretty obvious and profound. But how do you go about getting your foot in the door?

The Folly of Applications

I hope you understand that I am using a pen name in this book as I am divulging information that may potentially irritate some of the partners in the firm. I still love my career at consulting with PwC and have no intention to leave anytime soon. Using a pen name allows me to be "less political" in my language and share my true thoughts and observations as if I am speaking to you, instead of worrying about my career or potential lawsuits. However, if you have a desire to meet or contact me, please do so. At the end of this book, I will provide my e-mail address. I urge you to get in touch, shoot your questions to me, and I will be happy to respond at my earliest convenience!

I felt obliged to share insider information with people such as yourself so that you don't spend your most valuable asset, time, on going through website, job portals and crafting special CVs without hearing anything back. Analyzing a CV properly (looking for related experience, separating the good ones from the irrelevant ones, identifying BS) takes about 10 minutes. There are 480 minutes of work available per day. So, that means 1 person can analyze up to 48 CVs per day and it would take about

20 people to sort out only the initial resumes every day. Here is another interesting question for you. Can you guess how many recruitment personnel work at a regional HQ of PwC? The answer is a whopping number of four! Thus, it's mathematically impossible to actually read all the CVs submitted even in one day. I can hear you saying "there is computer software for this purpose which will sift through CVs based on certain keywords". Unfortunately, I can assure you that we don't rely on that sort of software, and I know for a fact that most other big consulting firm doesn't either.

Here below is the shocking truth; this is the number of recruitment personnel for offices with around 100 to 600 consultants:

Company	Number of Dedicated Recruitment Personnel
PwC	4
Deloitte	6
EY	3
KPMG	3
McKinsey	5
Strategy& (Formerly Booz)	4

Now you know for a fact that if you apply only at company portals that the most likely outcome is that you will never hear from the hiring manager. You may however get a call from a very junior HR analyst calling you for a "prescreening", which means you may actually have a 1% chance of an interview afterwards. And that will be entirely decided by how hard that junior employee pushes your resume to the senior HR

Manager, who will then have the opportunity to speak with the hiring partner. The odds are definitely stacked against you.

So in this book, I will talk about how you can increase your chances from near zero to about 20% to 50% depending on your communication skills and dedication. 50% chance for an interview with one of world's top consulting companies is one heck of a good chance!

CHAPTER THREE

Understanding Consultancy Firms and Preparing Yourself to Meet Their Needs

When applying for a consultancy, there are generally two scenarios in which you can successfully apply:

1. You are about to graduate from your undergrad degree, or from a business school

1.1. You are from a school that the consulting companies have identified as resource centers, i.e.; INSEAD for Strategy&, HBS for McK and BCG, etc.

1.2. You are from a school that has no ties with consulting firms.

2. You are an experienced hire, meaning you are probably an expert in a certain field.

The recommendations in this book will most likely add great value to both of these categories, either as an experienced hire or a recent graduate. But if you are already lucky enough to be studying at a resource center school, then you are ahead of all other applicants. You have a direct channel to introduce yourself to the firm, especially if you have a good GPA.

Let's jump to my high-level recommended approach. We will discuss these in more detail as we continue.

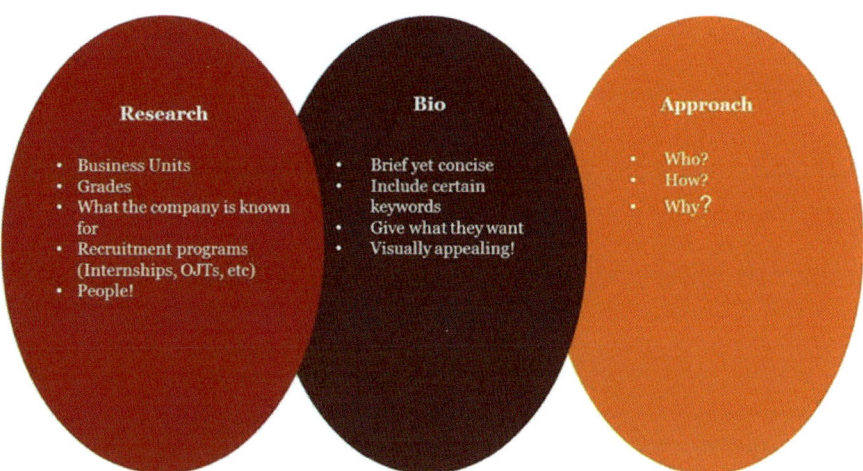

1. Research

1.1. Pick the Line of Service that has most consulting positions:

Every company has different departments, business units, teams, divisions, subdivisions, and grade levels. In my ten year consulting experience, I have yet to see two consultancy firms that have identical structures. This section will be tremendously important in your research. You will need to identify the business units that are under consulting for each firm, look at the supply of positions in those domains and then make your selection based on that. It's also important to take a look at their Line of Service as well. Sometimes there may be two lines of service for consulting industry. For example, PwC Consulting line of service has a business unit called Strategy consulting but also the firm has a separate

Consulting Interviews Guaranteed! 13

Line of Service for Strategy& that also delivers consulting engagements. You only have a few shots at making a proper introduction of yourself to the firm. You don't want to miss that shot by applying to a domain in which only PhDs are accepted with very limited supply of positions, unless of course you actually have a PhD and are considered to be the renowned individual in your domain.

Above is a graph showing you an overview of consulting by line of service/business units for the U.K. consultancy market.

Breakdown of the UK consulting market in 2014 (£m)		Growth rates 2014		
By service			**By sector**	
Technology	2,235	7.7%	Financial services	1,891	6.9%
Strategy	1,395	7.0%	Public sector	1,129	6.2%
Operational improvement	1,153	5.1%	Manufacturing	690	6.8%
			Technology, media and telecoms	653	4.8%
Financial management and risk	659	7.1%	Energy and resources	539	6.1%
HR and change management	577	4.8%	Services	474	5.8%
			Retail	253	9.7%
			Healthcare	197	8.4%
			Pharma and biotech	194	10.7%

This is an incredibly important graph. So if you apply for Healthcare, Biotech, Retail, Services and Energy consulting the odds are that you will have quite a hard time unless you are really the crème de la crème in your expertise. The sheer number of available spots just don't exist. The jobs available in consulting for Technology, Strategy, and Operational Improvement alone are higher than the next eleven lines of services combined. Although this data is for the UK consul-

The jobs available in consulting for Technology, Strategy, and Operational Improvement alone are higher than the next 11 lines of services combined

tancy market, this pattern will be repeated across multiple other regions.

The beauty of this data is that you most likely have a business background already, with a mix of technology. This will mean that you can pretty much choose most of the above fields as areas of expertise, or indeed lines of service. This will particularly apply if you are a recent graduate, and you will receive any training needed from these firms anyway. So if you choose the right domain for your application and back it up with the appropriate resume, you will significantly increase your chances as there will be more supply. I can hear you saying that there is also high competition. Trust me…the lesser the supply the higher the requirements are for candidates, and there are significantly less opportunities for only "good" candidates. So make sure you target the Business Unit and Line of Service that are suitable to your skillsets with the largest supply of positions available. By applying to Technology Consulting instead of Retail you are increasing your chances by 10 fold!

1.2. Identify the Business Units in each firm

Now I am going to need you to create an Excel list with business units per company to which you will later submit applications. This will be of tremendous help once we start making the applications. It's critical that you understand what business units exist in each firm.

Do you already see what we are getting at? You need to choose a business line from each company you want to work at. While making the selection, you need to look at their consulting position supply. The more the merrier. Later on when we approach people, you need to be able to say why you want that particular business unit. By taking this approach, you will actually reach the very company that requires staff in the very department that you're targeting, not an application that goes straight to the junk box of recruiters.

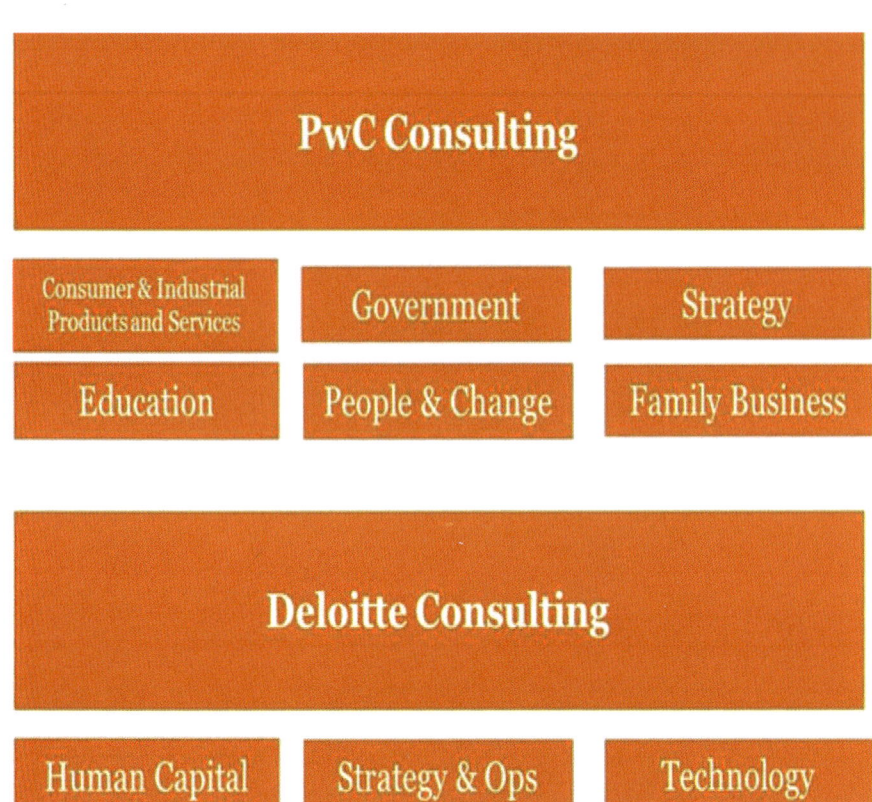

1.3. Understand the Area of expertise for each firm

Each consulting company specializes, or is at least known as an expert, in one particular field. Their area of expertise at a first glance may look as if it overlaps, but in reality they are all known for one thing to be perfect at carrying out. This will help you later on during the development of your resume as well as guessing the supply of roles.

For example, if you have a very high technology background then PwC may not be the perfect employer for you. We don't get as many technology projects as Deloitte. Or if you are a niche strategy formulator, you should look at strategy firms like McKinsey, Strategy& (a PwC Subsidiary now), Monitor (a Deloitte Subsidiary), or boutique firms like Roland Berger. So, it's important to highlight the elements in your resume that cater to what the company actually needs. And the need fundamentally comes from the projects they win and deliver. As EY, KPMG, rarely get jobs in strategy formulation and execution, there is no need for them to hire staff heavily for those units. Thus, they look for talent with skillsets suitable for the projects they win. The chart below will help you understand what these companies really specialize in, hence what delivers most of their revenues, and where they recruit the most people in their respective specialty domains. In simple terms, they hire most people in the domains they win most projects. Making an application for a supply chain strategy role in PwC may not get you anywhere as much as applying to the same role in Accenture.

We know which lines of services employ most consultants, and which firms specialize in which niche, and hence potentially employs the most consultants. Simply by knowing and understanding these two inputs, we have already increased our chances dramatically.

Company	Known for
PwC	Strategy Execution, Implementation, PMO, Process improvement
Deloitte	Technology deployment, It transformation
EY	Performance improvement company transformation

While we're on the topic, I'd also urge you to read more about the firm you are applying to if you want to sustain. You need to understand what separates one from another. McKinsey has been able to create a very strong name amongst the MBAs. You need to carefully think whether it's a company for you. I have worked with McK consultants for years on joint projects. I cannot tell you how many times they have approached me and my team members for a job. Not because of the tough working conditions or long hours either. The kind of job McK offers is very similar in nature. You may be looking at different companies and sectors, but most of the time it is a strategy development. Essentially, you will be following a similar methodology which applies to most situations, for pretty much all industries. Based on my observations, it gets boring for many consultants very quickly and incredibly tiring, leading to burn-outs. A

Consulting Interviews Guaranteed! 17

typical strategy development engagement lasts anywhere between three and eight weeks (depending on the scope). That means you will be jumping from client to client every month doing pretty much the same thing.

After some time, this will get really tiring and you will crave for long-term client engagements which companies like McK, Roland Berger, and BCG rarely win. Long-term engagements are mostly with companies like PwC and Deloitte Consulting, who are known to be implementers.

So what will generally happen is that McK comes in, develops the strategy and hands it over to PwC to implement. Implementation can take anything from a one month to a year or even longer. By this process, you maximize the stability and lessons learned, get to know people and your client, enjoy working with your team that have just mobilized for the project, and still short enough of an engagement to always keep you motivated.

McK, BCG, and Roland Berger are all great firms, but they are in a field that can get very challenging for the consultant. Not because of the job nature alone, but rather the time you are forced to spend on each client. McKinsey also has a very high turnover rate compared to other firms. Once again, these are all great firms. But you just need to make sure it is for you. One McK consultant recently told me that in order to survive at the firm, you need to be a sprinter running a marathon with 10 seconds breaks every 10 hours. I know I can't do that! I need a good rest after every sprint. Or I can run a marathon with no rest. But not both!

At PwC Consulting, we work very hard as well but it's rare we work until 9, 10 pm and at weekends. Usually, the work is over for us after 6 pm, we start planning for the next day and sometimes just wait for the client to leave. This usually translates to a 7pm finish at the latest. Here is the difference, though during the day, we make sure that we work very hard and smart and eliminate all forms of procrastination and time-wasting. Since we are incredibly efficient at what we do, our nine hour work day is normally a 90 hour work week for teams in other non-consulting firms.

1.3. Prepare the list of people who work in field you chose

Luckily, for you, today everyone is accessible. There is this tremendous tool available to everyone, called; LinkedIn. It's such an incredible website that gives you access to whomever you want to reach. Again, I can hear you saying "I have done it before, and nobody responds". Of course they won't, that is because you are not approaching LinkedIn correctly. You are not showing them any 'opportunity'. We will cover that later in our methods section. But for now, all you need to do is, again go back to your sweet old Excel file, and make a template something similar to below.

Firm	Department	Business Unit	Grade	Name	Surname	Linkedin Account
PwC	Consulting	Government	Partner	xxx	xxx	xxx
	Consulting	Government	Director	xxx	xxx	xxx
Deloitte	Consulting	Technology	Partner	xxx	xxx	xxx

All you need is to spend an hour to list the names of all the people, with their LinkedIn accounts, in the departments you will later apply to.

It's fairly simple. Please fight the urge to send messages to them at this stage. We will cover how to do that in due course.

So we have now made the first stage of the application process, the next step is to set up your bio.

Consulting Interviews Guaranteed!

CHAPTER FOUR

Creating a Biography and LinkedIn Profile

Preparation of Bio

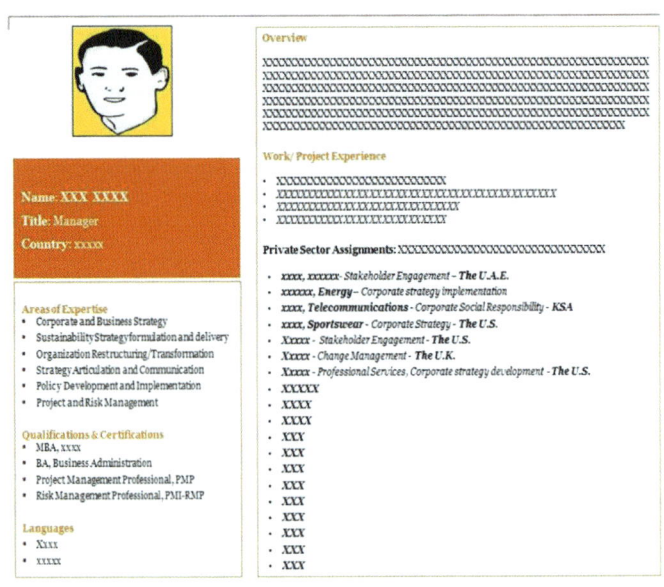

When you are preparing a new resume, it's best to start from scratch. I will need you to prepare two resumes, one bio out of a simple PowerPoint slide, and one on LinkedIn. For your PowerPoint (or PDF) bio, you may use a template as previous page;

As you can see, the template only highlights the important things that people are particularly interested in reading. Although being a socially active person who participates in social activities and sports is great, this is extraneous information at this stage. Consultancies would rather hear about this in person. Well written one page biography is all you need, along with a well-crafted LinkedIn resume. It will soon become clear why LinkedIn is important for our approach.

While preparing your profile, I'd like to urge you to look at some of the megatrends as well. Consultants are constantly on the look out for talent that has exposure in emerging megatrends. Since most consultants have been doing their jobs for a long time, they sometimes rely on newcomers to have experience in this area. If you can highlight some of them in your resume, this will amount to an extra 5% credit for you. The graphs here are just quick snapshots of emerging megatrends. But if you break each one down you will find out which skillsets are related to each, for example:

- Sustainability Reporting in accordance with Global

- Reporting Initiative,

- Controls, compliance, governance

- Maturity assessment for project management methodologies

It is important that you do not rush this step. Take your time composing every single sentence that you write. This is only a one-page bio or a short LinkedIn profile so please spend a sufficient amount of time to make sure that you mostly comply with the following structure;

You have accomplished Y, following the approach of X, measured by Z.

Consulting Interviews Guaranteed!

This structure will not fit for every single sentence, but you should utilise it as often as possible. Once you finish your one-page bio, you can now start preparing your professional LinkedIn profile.

There are many resources available regarding how to prepare a LinkedIn profile and what to focus on. So I would prefer to steer clear of that. The list of resources are too long, so I would prefer not to attempt to link to, or reference, some here. I am sure you will find excellent resources; they are certainly easily available.

However, the important thing that I will mention is that you must take the following steps:

Small details in resume preparation matter. If the perfect resume is rated at 100 points, you can get 15 points from formatting alone. It's crucial in order to attract consultancies for you to present information in a visually appealing way. I have to admit, there is more than one occasion where the content of a presentation that I have delivered to a client wasn't up to my usual standards, but the visual aspects were so good that the client left the presentation extremely impressed. So make sure your bio and LinkedIn profile is as good looking as it can be.

You can get another 5 points from use of excellent language, 20 points from impactful experiences conveyed beautifully. Perhaps another 20 from either former employers or business schools that furnishes you with more credibility and reputation. These are of course very qualitative. It's a numbers game at the end of the day. Just try collecting points from here and there, and your bio will serve its purpose when you finally reach out to the people you listed above. Don't do it yet, though. Next we will look at whom you need to approach.

CHAPTER FIVE

Approaching Consultancies

Now this is probably the most critical segment of this book. We will discuss who and how to approach for a job application in order to get an interview

HR Myths

You will first need to forget about applying on the company website, or approaching HR elsewhere. Contrary to what you may believe, HR is not the complete recruiting arm of these firms. It's not that they don't do recruitment, but it's not their priority to process online applications, even though they post job ads. I know, I know…they do however go through every single CV in great detail if it's referred by an insider, especially if that insider is a manager and above the level of consultant.

Contrary to what their title suggests, they are not in the firm to "recruit". They are employed to keep a master database of the candidates with certain skillsets, arrange interviews with hiring managers, and sometimes conduct HR orientation internally. That's about it. So they are not really your key stakeholder. Never be rude to them, of course, but they are just simply not your target audience. Approaching a recruiter on LinkedIn, or networking events won't get you very far.

A typical recruiter, no matter how senior their grade is, has very limited information about consulting, or the type of skillsets that are in play, other than a bunch of books that they may have read about psychology, which most of the time doesn't apply to consulting. They are experts at categorizing people as Pink character, Y Character and whatever other methods they may subscribe to, but clueless about the skillsets needed for a benchmark study, strategy framework development, project implementation, process improvement, and all the other hardcore skillsets that we will actually need in order to succeed.

This would not be highly worrying to me if they could actually get the other 50% right by effectively evaluating the soft skillsets. However, even that is very much a grey area. The type of characters we need for consulting don't really exist elsewhere in corporates. Therefore, the books written about those soft skills may not necessarily always apply.

The Over-Ambitious Mistake

Another danger of recruiters and HR getting heavily engaged in recruitment and orientation is that they over-estimate the importance of being ambitious and extremely driven. In reality, a great consultant offers everything in moderation. Over-ambitious people tend to step on the toes of others, become arrogant, and close their ears to the clients' input. That's a career killer.

We are not looking for lions, super leaders who always take the initiative, never stop talking, apparently in a perpetual battle to take leadership in meetings. I am sure you have heard of many people like this. Let me tell you the outcome of a situation similar to this that I observed very closely in my career. They are so driven and brainwashed that they forget to actually listen to, and work together with the client. They think they are experts and have to know the best, even better than the person who has done that job for decades. 80% of the time they make fools out of themselves. When it gets out of hand, clients ask them to leave the meeting room, and then send stinky emails to the engagement partner. Your client is not stupid. The very fact that they are paying millions of dollars for a couple of months work means they are smart enough to look for value, and how to measure the outcome. This particular occurrence is a very common problem with one consulting firm that I can't name on this occasion, so it is certainly something of which you should be aware.

Initiating the Job

You need to look at how the job need is initiated. This is illustrated below:

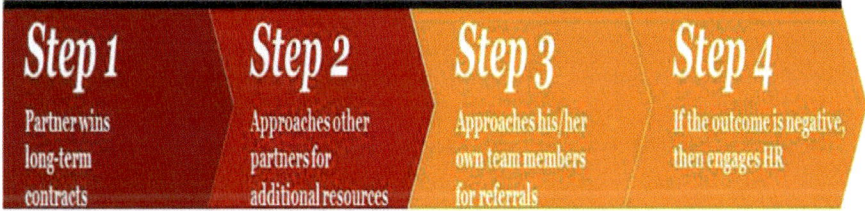

Because HR is almost never prepared to give resumes that meet the needs of the partner, this step is usually extremely lengthy and most of the time position is again filled by referral.

Step 3 and 4 is the time when the partner is most vulnerable. He needs to staff the team as quickly as possible as the project start date nears. That's the time that referrals from his own team members are immediately interviewed and hired in a span of one to two weeks. That's when you will need to make sure that your resume is in their hands.

Partners in big consulting firms are extremely busy professionals. They are constantly working to win new projects, review the deliverables of on-going projects, team staffing, budget work, and future planning. The odds are that if you get in touch with them they won't even read your message. The people you are going to need to approach are Managers or Directors. These people will be more approachable and have a few minutes to actually meet with you. It's all about how you approach them, though.

LinkedIn InMails

Assuming that you have already created your one-page bio and an impeccable LinkedIn profile, you can now go ahead and purchase your "InMails". If you are not familiar with this, it is LinkedIn's messaging service that enables you to send an email to anyone without the need to be connected to them. The good thing about this service is that you can also track whether and when they opened and read your message. If you don't get a response back within a certain time, LinkedIn will actually credit back your account. It is also very important to note here that please do not ever send a connection request. This will only harm your chances. When you approach through InMail, they actually know that you paid to deliver that message across, and that you really want it. The least they will do is respond with a negative. But chances are that they will fully read what you wrote and possibly give you a shot.

You can now revisit the list of people you created per company and per division. You will send an introductory email to only one person in your chosen business unit per company. So, if you are applying to four, you can send four emails to four people you find most approachable in those business units. You should allow up to three days for them to respond after you see the "read" status from LinkedIn. If they don't then do not change the business unit, but change the person that you contact within the same business unit. You should repeat this process until you get a favourable outcome. The important thing, however, is the message you convey and what motivators exist for the person you contact to meet you or speak with you on the phone. Let's look at these motivations broadly:

Referral Bonus	• Almost all consulting firms have a referral bonus that pays anywhere between USD 1,000 to USD 3,000 depending on the position and company. A referrer can make up to USD 3,000 just by entertaining your request, meeting with you and sending a simple e-mail to his/her partner. That will be the easiest money he/she makes if you get the job. I referred over 10 people so far and 4 of them have been successfully employed. All I did was sending out a simple e-mail. That was it.
Opportunity to work with someone who is motivated and loyal	• It's easy to guess that someone you refer into the organization will stay loyal to you. You need to understand that world of consulting can sometimes turn into tug of war. There is always competition not between firms but also between consultants. It's always good to know that you will have another soldier in the battle if you need to. In addition, it's always great to know that this new hire will work extra hard for you to make sure you don't regret your decision, of referring him allowing the manager to deliver quality work for the client.
Threat of someone getting in to the firm that he/she didn't help	• The opposite of the above scenario is that you don't respond to the e-mails or phone calls of the candidate who is approaching you and he/she actually ends up in the firm hating you from day one. Imagine what an awkward situation it will be. "Hey John Doe, do you remember me? I am the guy that you didn't even bother to respond to at LinkedIn. Now, we are colleagues." Never pleasant.
Opportunity to feel important	• The final motivator is very simple and can be tied to our very basic psychological need; being appreciated and looked up to. You say a few words that what an amazing professional he must be to be working at such a prestigious company, he will immediately raise the white flag and welcome you with a sentence "tell me more".

Somehow people who don't work for major consulting / tech / investment firms think that these companies are so advanced that their processes are no longer driven by humans. Instead, it is expected that computers, process maps, and other automated procedures govern everything that goes in these firms, which includes recruitment as well. The reality is very different. It's all about humans. The quality work they do, the problems they encounter, the jealousy, over-competitiveness, burn-outs; these are all human related. So is the recruitment. If your resume contributes 50% towards your success, the other 50% comes from your character.

Consulting Interviews Guaranteed!

Can companies get along with you? Will you follow their lead? Will you challenge people enough? Are you smart? Can you solve problems? Can you commit to working long hours when needed? Will you step up without being asked? Trust me, these are incredibly important elements of any application and character, and you can give hints of these in your approach with LinkedIn Inmail or at a short discussion in a networking event, and then seal it in the interview.

Nobody has the perfect bio/resume. But if you have one that is good enough and then possess the other soft skills required, then you do have a good shot.

CHAPTER SIX
What to do and What Not to do

I will now share with you some of the ridiculous referral requests I have received over the past few months alone, and then we can analyze them together, identify the lessons learned, then craft the perfect e-mail eventually. Sounds good? Read on...

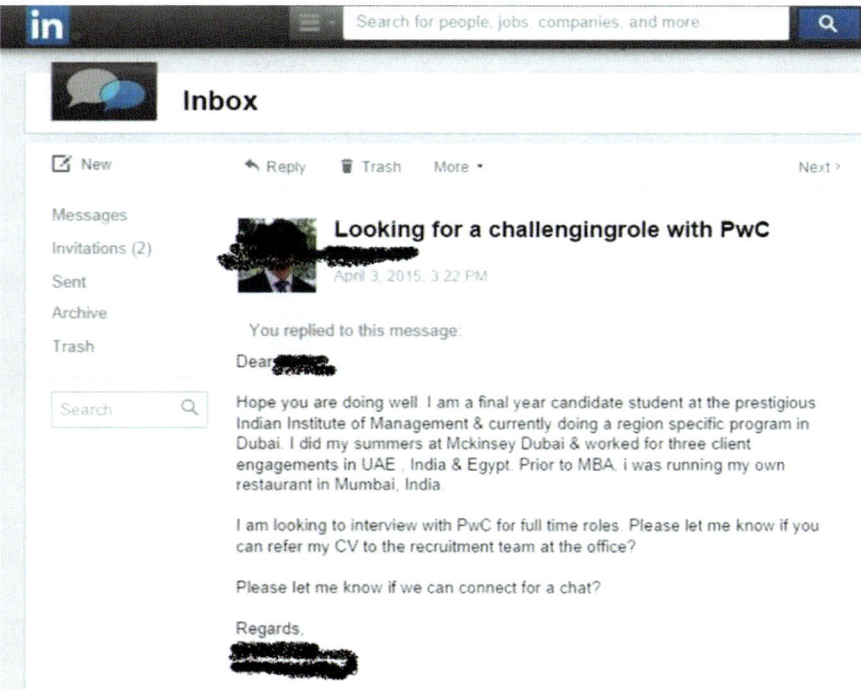

Let me quickly share with you why I didn't refer this candidate;

1. There is an error in the subject line; "challenging role".

2. Use of "&", did my "summers"

3. It's not Mckinsey but it's McKinsey. The least you can do is to spell your former employer's name correctly.

4. Not "i" but "I".

5. "Prior to MBA, I was running my own restaurant in Mumbai, India" Good for you! If you haven't noticed,

1) This is not India, 2) We are not in the restaurant business at PwC. So what is relevant in that message that gives you credibility? Answer… nothing!

6. "I am looking to interview with PwC for full time roles". Of course you are. And we feel honored you chose us, sir!

7. "Please let me know if we can connect for a chat?" Why would I do that? Oh, sorry, because you are looking to interview with PwC… Silly me. Let's chat then bro!

I am sharing these because, I actually find it unethical for people to just blurt out a message with no prior thinking, planning, or even minor research. These kinds of e-mails will not get you anywhere.

How about another example? It's fun, isn't it?

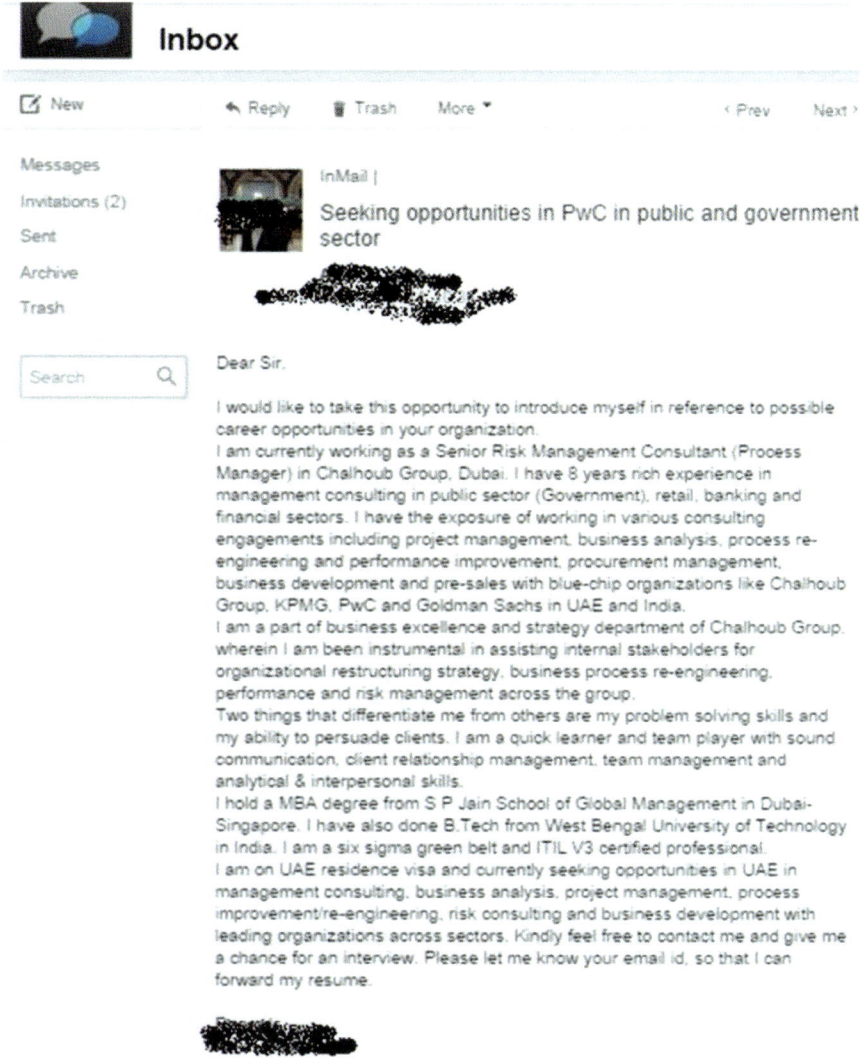

Let's start!

1. I am not a sir. I am a 34 year old young man! I actually have a name, but since you are copying and pasting this message to everyone, you didn't bother to make that small change. Calling me a sir was the easiest choice.

Consulting Interviews Guaranteed!

2. So, let's look at the career fields you are looking to get into once more; "management consulting, business analysis, project management, process improvement and re-engineering, risk consulting, business development with leading organizations across sectors". Can you perhaps be more specific and at least show the courtesy of mentioning the company name you are applying to?

3. The worst of all is that when I checked the LinkedIn profile of this candidate, I wasn't able to see any of the employer names he mentioned in his e-mail.

Now, let's look at some of the things a good e-mail should possess;

1. Human touch. You need to make me think that you crafted this e-mail for me. You actually took the time to personalize the email, mention my name, business unit, and company name. You can perhaps look at my LinkedIn profile and then throw out some complements, or at least indicate how you hope to follow a similar career path by taking certain steps.

2. Do your research first. As we covered in this book extensively, it is of vital importance to determine which business unit you are targeting, to identify the people or LinkedIn in that unit, to develop your profile accordingly with keywords specific to that field…and only then can you actually approach someone. Because the first thing they will do is to check your LinkedIn profile for relevant experience.

3. Don't ask for them to refer you. Ask for an opportunity to discuss consulting as a career for you, and share your desire to benefit from their vast experience and guidance. Trust me…this will work. This should be considered an absolutely essential point. Make them feel important! Make them feel as if they are someone whom you really look up to. Make them feel that you would die for a 30 minute discussion with them. Make them feel that speaking to them would be a life-altering experience! Just pamper their ego. But…don't go too far, don't be excessive and sycophantic. The tone of your message should clearly show that you are self-confident, assertive, and open to learn from the best.

4. Make sure you stick to a maximum of five to 10 sentences. I guarantee you that they will look at your LinkedIn profile. Think of it as a phishing tool. You want them to be interested enough to look at your profile, you don't want to copy your profile into the e-mail. If they are interested, they will get back to you and agree to have a cup of coffee or a 10 minute phone discussion.

5. Don't send InMail to members of the same business unit. We are trying to create trust here, so your trust will be damaged if you send an InMail to multiple people and they find out about it at their lunch break. These people are very well connected through the business world and use LinkedIn very heavily to keep in touch with their formal clients. Therefore if you don't get a response in 2 days this is almost certainly because they are not interested. So don't pester people unnecessarily, this will damage your application.

6. Follow up your initial application. The reason why you follow up is because you want to make them acutely aware that it was not an InMail sent out of the blue. You want to indicate that you genuinely want to learn from them and highly value their opinion. No-one will want to take the risk of referring someone that they don't know. So you are merely asking for a cup of coffee at their convenience, maybe during their lunch break, possibly a pint of beer after work, joining them in their sports activities, or inviting them to a networking event that you happen to know about which is also potentially beneficial to their line of business. In short, keep it relatively informal at this stage.

7. If you still receive no response after two days, then move on to the next person in the same business unit. Repeat this until you exhaust all your resources or get a positive response and then move to the next business unit. You can follow this process for all the consulting firms you apply to in parallel. It will work!

Now, let's look at an example,

Hi Jane,

My name is John Doe. I'm a young, enthusiastic MBA grad from xxx who just moved to xxx. I've been following your LinkedIn posts for a while now, and was wondering if you could spare 10 minutes of your time for me where I can perhaps have the opportunity to learn from your experience in consulting? I would also love to hear about how you made the transition from xxx to xxx as a fresh graduate, and any advice you may have regarding consulting in xxx business unit. I am very excited to learn from the best. If you have some time in the next couple of weeks I'd love to invite you for a cup of coffee anytime at your convenience!

Thanks in advance,

John

That is the sort of tone and length you are looking for. Short, snappy, to the point, and not at all presumptuous. It sets up the possibility of an informal meeting, and makes it clear that you value the opinion of the person you have contacted. This approach ticks all the boxes, and is ultimately gold dust.

Networking

In my experience, most of my mentees have landed interviews by simply following the above approach; research the industry and business units for application, research the people who currently work in those fields, create a LinkedIn bio, approach through LinkedIn InMail, and finish with a phone call or a cup of coffee/pint of beer. However, there is nothing stopping you from exploring the other high result producing method that is networking. Networking is definitely one of the greatest tools you have to introduce yourself to consultants. Once you make a good impression to managers and above grades, that's all you need to get your foot in the door. It's just that short impression of 5 to 10 minutes. Forget about case studies, lengthy essay preparations, and all other formalities. Here are some key points for effective networking;

- Don't be too eager. Wait for the opportunity to present itself.

- Don't speak too much, listen more.

- Ask questions; but not to prove that you are smart or attempting to beat the consultant with your intellectual capacity, but to actually learn about the industry, the way they work, and the challenges they face.

- Don't sell your background to them. There is nothing to pitch here. They will ask you if they are interested. Just act normal, smart, intellectual…ultimately, be yourself.

- You need to make a good impression right there and seal it with action. They probably won't respond to you once you send them an e-mail afterwards, that's if you are even lucky enough to get his business card.

- Show them an opportunity, or at least make sure they benefit from the conversation. For example, I was recently at a networking event at Cass Business School and was speaking with the current students about Greece's economic turmoil and about the Prime Minister Tsipras. There was a gentleman in the group who taught me something I didn't know, it was about a potential credit deal he was pursuing with Russia, and was citing the outcome of Tsipras' meeting with Putin. I was impressed and I remember the name of that gentleman just for the sheer reason that he taught me something that I wanted to know.

- I don't think there is a universal preference for junior consultants to be introvert or extrovert. At least, I haven't come across anything related to it. But looking at the junior consultants, analysts, I realize that the vast majority of them are introverts with good communication skills. I haven't seen many extroverts at junior positions. But the funny thing is, most managers and partners are extroverts. I don't know if the introverts convert to extroverts as they progress in their careers or the extroverts get to be promoted higher. This is just my observation. I am not telling you to act like an introvert if you are applying for a junior position and act like an extrovert if you are applying for a senior position. But I am certainly not saying not to either. Just sharing an observation.

You also need to remember that each interaction with the firm can either lend you credit or make you lose credit. Make sure you are prepared fully. You don't want to burn bridges. There was a time when I was so irritated by the lack of professionalism of another consultant who had applied to PwC Consulting that I personally took the liberty to block his application. He was sharing very confidential information about his previous clients with his current firm with me, a competitor of that firm. This is a big no-no in consulting. If we employed that guy, we would have no guarantee he wouldn't do the same. And I am sure he did it for the 'right reasons'; purely to keep me happy and give me some insider information that can potentially help with my work. But there are always professional boundaries. You may talk about your manager, your firm and your policies, but you do not divulge critical information about your client; especially if it's a publicly traded one then it's even a criminal offense!

If you are participating in an event where a consultant is making a presentation, ask something publicly! Make sure your question is smart, and that you are genuinely trying to learn the answer. Don't try to beat the consultant or ask a question that puts him in a difficult position in front of an audience.

Once the event is over, go back to the presenter and ask a follow-up question. This is by far the easiest way to make an impression that lasts a long time. He will remember you…just make sure that you are asking questions that it is for the right reasons!

To ensure success, you can prepare in advance. You already know in advance the topic and the presenter. Just go to your best friend Google and research about the topic, find something that has happened recently, and important enough to discuss this publicly. Nothing beats preparation. Then, when the time comes, ask your smart question and make sure it was not answered in his presentation. It would be a career killer if he starts his answer by: "As I mentioned earlier in my presentation…" Oopps!

You can even ask professional questions related to his successes provided that you researched him/her well enough to know the details. I have said this many times, but once again consultants love to think they are the best of the management world, and nothing beats talking about your successes publicly in front of an audience. Give them the opportunity to do this!

Follow up Email

Finally, I know every book you read tells you to send that good old thank you email the very next day. Well, it's not that simple actually. A thank you letter that you send gives nothing to the other person other than a meaningless bunch of words haphazardly put together, which are then sent across to his office. If the subject line is "Thank you", he probably won't even read it unless you made a quite considerable impression.

My suggestion is that you add value. Why not throw in a key statistic that you found about the topic you were discussing a day earlier? Why not actually pay for that resource if it's a paid one which shows your commitment? Why not gift a book about that topic through Amazon? Find something that adds value. That's the kind of thank you letter that will leave a long lasting impression!

CONCLUSION

Everything about this book has been about finding relatively unconventional methods to get that first step. So take your time to make sure that you truly give them something they need. There is no rush. You don't have to send that email first thing in the morning. You can send it later in the week. I am sure the person in question has good enough of a memory to remember you even after a month. If they haven't shared their business card, then as I covered earlier, go purchase a LinkedIn InMail and reach out to them through this platform.

Thanks for reading my book. Now you need to go out there and get it done.

The recommendations in this will only work if you are truly committed to it. You need to make sure you take one step at a time. Your failure to get that interview will be mine so if you are confused about any of the recommendations or need further advise, why don't you shoot me an email with your questions, or just to say hi at landinginterviews@yahoo.com. I'd love to hear from you! If my time permits, I can also conduct mock interviews if you actually landed interviews following my methods. I am here to help and your success is the greatest satisfaction I can get out of writing this book. I am obviously not looking to get rich by this book priced at USD 2.99 so let me at least get the satisfaction of helping people.

Printed in Great Britain
by Amazon